✶ THE ✶
AMERICAN FLAG

★ THE ★
AMERICAN FLAG

FRIEDMAN/FAIRFAX

A FRIEDMAN/FAIRFAX BOOK

© 1998 by Michael Friedman Publishing Group, Inc.

Second Friedman/Fairfax edition 2001

Please visit our website: www.metrobooks.com

Library of Congress Cataloging-in-Publication Data available upon request.

ISBN 1-56799-660-4

Editor: Celeste Sollod
Art Director: Jeff Batzli
Designer: Andrea Karman
Photography Editors: Karen Barr and Wendy Missan

Printed in the U.S.A.

3 5 7 9 10 8 6 4 2

Distributed by Sterling Publishing Company, Inc.
387 Park Avenue South
New York, NY 10016
Distributed in Canada by Sterling Publishing
Canadian Manda Group
One Atlantic Avenue, Suite 105
Toronto, Ontario, Canada M6K 3E7
Distributed in Australia by
Capricorn Link (Australia) Pty, Ltd.
P.O. Box 704, Windsor, NSW 2756 Australia

This flag, which we honor and under which we serve, is the emblem of our unity, our power, our thought and purpose as a nation. It has no other character than that which we give it from generation to generation. The choices are ours.

Woodrow Wilson

Our True Flag

A piece of blue cloth. Seven strips of red fabric and six strips of white. Fifty white stars. Some thread. Is it possible that such simple things can move a million hearts to admiration, even awe; can provoke a million words of rhetoric and poetry; can express pride, hope, joy, and even anger? Yes: such has been—and is—the power of the American flag.

Flags, banners, and standards have always been powerful symbols, of course. The Bible speaks of setting up "an ensign for the nations" (Isaiah 11:12), of a splendid vision "terrible as an army with banners" (Song of Solomon 6:10), and of "every man in his place by their standards" (Numbers 2:17). Other civilizations and societies have recognized the power of these emblems, but few have raised their flags, literally and figuratively, as high as the Stars and Stripes.

The Birth of the Stars and Stripes

How did this extraordinary transformation of pieces of colored cloth into a great symbol take place? The flags of Denmark, Armenia, and Ethiopia, among others, are supposed to have been divinely inspired, but Americans take pride in

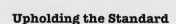

having created their own banner. Starting from very prosaic and practical necessities, elaborating usage and meaning over time, they associated the flag with each national victory—and national trauma—thereby advancing Old Glory to its present revered position.

The colors are those of England (red and white) and Scotland (blue and white), long familiar to early colonists along the Eastern seaboard. The origins of the Stars and Stripes are rooted in both respect for and rebellion against British tradition. British sailors put the Union Jack in the upper hoist corner—the "canton"—of a flag whose background was either plain or striped. The banner of the radical Sons of Liberty, an organization that raised the first organized protests against British misrule, consisted of thirteen stripes for the colonies united in defense of American liberties.

Our first national flag, the Continental Colors, joined those stripes with a Union Jack canton, symbolizing the (vain) hope of Americans prior to the Declaration of Independence that King George III would recognize the legitimacy of their claims. General George Washington ordered the Continental Colors hoisted on January 1, 1776, to honor the creation of the Continental army, and a ship flying the Continental Colors received a salute on November 16 of that year from a Dutch fortress in the Caribbean, stirring American pride in the recognition awarded their new independence.

Later, the Union Jack on the Continental Colors was replaced with thirteen stars, symbolic of the United States as "a new constellation," an equal among nations. Congress adopted this design—the first Stars and Stripes—on June 14, 1777. During the Revolution, that banner not only played a practical, identifying role on ships and forts, it also established itself among the men and women who had created the new nation in a way that no other country's flag had ever done. This was no royal banner of an arbitrary monarch, no religious emblem of an established creed, no autocratic heraldry of an oppressive ruling class, no proclamation of racial or ideological purity. Created by and for the people, the Stars and Stripes would henceforth enfold every American.

Upholding the Standard

Twice in the succeeding century, when the flag and the very country it stood for were threatened, millions rallied to its cause in great ways and small, ensuring that "our flag was still there." Francis Scott Key wrote those stirring words during the War of 1812 as part of his poem "The Defense of Fort McHenry," during the British bombardment threatening Baltimore. Set to a well-known melody, Key's patriotic poem became the national anthem, "The Star-Spangled Banner." Our "Second War of Independence," as the War of 1812 is also called, saw nearby Washington

D.C. burned, but in the end both the nation and its flag—by then, with fifteen stars and fifteen stripes, one of each for each of the states—were preserved.

Two generations later, the Confederate States of America was proclaimed under the Stars and Bars, a flag clearly inspired by the Stars and Stripes that it replaced. The resulting Civil War proved to be a great turning point in American history—for the Constitution, for human rights, for unity, and for the flag that symbolized the once-more United States. No community of the North or the South could ever forget the half million who died defending the principles they felt to be incarnated in their respective battle-borne flags.

Thenceforth, no American would be the property of another, nor would any portion of the country declare itself a new nation under its own flag. Political differences, sectional rivalries, economic disparities, and other issues of great import would be freely and fairly debated thereafter under the all-embracing banner: the Stars and Stripes.

The Flag Today

As the vibrant young country expanded, a star and stripe were added for each new state, but it was soon obvious that the added stripes would ruin the appearance of the banner. The third Stars and Stripes, adopted in 1817, went back to the thirteen stripes found in the original flag, honoring the original thirteen states that started our union, but it was decided to add a star for each new state that joined those already united.

Over the succeeding decades, the Stars and Stripes achieved a popularity as great in peacetime as it had known in war. Heralded in song and poetry, in painting, sculpture, and drama, the American flag has found its way into sports events, churches, schools, and homes. Hearts beat with pride on seeing the flag displayed everywhere from country lanes to city plazas. Displayed to show the American people's pride in their country and its freedom, Old Glory is a tangible sign that cries out, "Let freedom ring."

Popular indignation has led to laws against physical manipulation, including destruction, of the flag as "desecration," but ultimately the increased use of the flag and its image—even in tasteless or shocking ways—only proves its enduring symbolic force, as more Americans associate themselves with its highest ideals. In stark contrast, few foreign powers—even the parliamentary democracies of Europe—can claim such widespread attachment to their official flags.

In the twentieth century, the United States has experienced economic depression and civil disorders; confronted its own racism, sexism, and other limitations; and engaged in wars against totalitarian regimes abroad. Through it all, the Stars and Stripes has not only survived, but has taken on greater meaning, as our once fledgling nation has come of age. Our flag is more highly and widely respected, more frequently displayed, better understood than it ever has been before. How is this possible? How can an eighteenth-century banner enter the twenty-first century with such great confidence?

The secret lies in the liberties that Americans and others see incarnated in the daily life of the land—its courts, its marketplace, its schools and churches, its families and friendships. Like the Constitution, the flag stands for a few bedrock principles and for the potential of each citizen to realize his or her dreams within those broad limits. Ultimately no weapon, army, material wealth, or size of territory or of population guarantees our flag. Our principles—and above all our lives as free people existing under just laws—must always be recognized as our true flag, embodied in but not limited to the fifty stars, the thirteen stripes, and the red, white, and blue of Old Glory.

Whitney Smith, Ph.D.
Flag Research Center
Winchester, MA
December 17, 1997

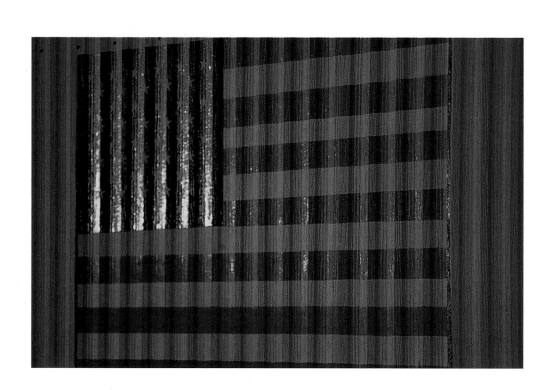

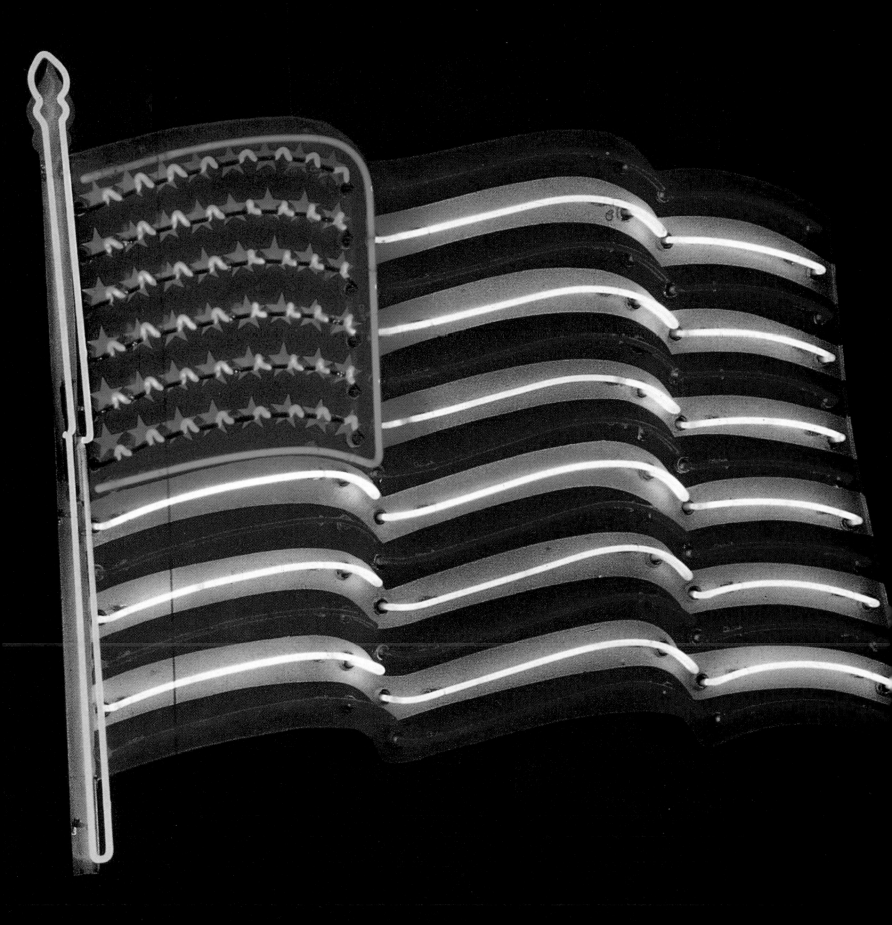

PHOTO CREDITS